Hamza Learns About Religions

By Ameena Chaudhry

ISBN 978-0-9739778-5-1
Published in Canada by iPromote Media Inc.

It was a beautiful day as Hamza was walking home after school with his friend
David. David was very excited that he was going to be getting a lot of presents
because Christmas was fast approaching.

David continued talking about all the presents he wanted for Christmas. Once Hamza reached his house and said goodbye to David, he thought to himself how lucky David was to be getting many presents during the Christmas holidays.

"Assalamalakum Mama, I'm home," Hamza said as he walked through the front door. He gave his Mama a big hug and his mother noticed that Hamza looked really excited. "You sure seem to be in a good mood today Hamza," Mama said. Hamza replied, "I have a great idea, let's celebrate Christmas this year like David."

Mama walked over and sat on the sofa in front of Hamza. "As Muslims, we do not celebrate Christmas," Mama explained.   Hamza's mood quickly changed as he did not like what he was hearing.

Getting very upset, Hamza threw his cap on the ground and started crying. He really wanted to celebrate Christmas like the other children at school. He thought it was unfair that he wasn't going to get any presents at Christmas.

Hearing all the commotion, Hamza's Papa and sister Aisha came running into the room. "What seems to be the matter, why is Hamza so upset?" asked Papa. Hamza's mother explained to Papa and Aisha that Hamza wanted to celebrate Christmas.

Very upset, Hamza stomped out of the family room and ran up the stairs to his bedroom crying.

Later that evening, Grandpa came by to visit the family. When Grandpa found out why Hamza was upset, he explained to Hamza about Christmas and other religious holidays.

"Your friend David celebrates Christmas because he is a Christian. As Muslims we celebrate two Eid holidays and from what I remember you got a lot of presents last Eid," said Grandpa.

Hamza remembered that his family had celebrated Eid-ul-Fitr and Eid-ul-Adha just recently and he got a lot of presents during those two holidays.

"Hamza, many people in the world have different religions and celebrate different events," explained Grandpa. "You don't need to worry about not getting presents on Christmas because you will always have your own holidays."

Grandpa went on to explain to Hamza that people have different religions and beliefs and that we should respect each other's differences.

"Your friend David will spend time with his family on Christmas and get presents. When the next Eid comes, you will also celebrate with your family and get gifts," commented Grandpa.

Hamza felt much better after talking with his Grandpa about why he was upset. Grandpa then tucked Hamza into bed.

"I wonder what other holidays my friends celebrate," Hamza thought to himself.

The next day at school, Hamza started to look for his friends at break because he was curious to learn what other holidays they celebrated.

Hamza walked over to the swings and saw his friend Jacob. "Hey Jacob, do you celebrate a special religious holiday?" asked Hamza. "I celebrate Hanukkah because I am Jewish," replied Jacob.

Hamza saw his friend Suneel on the slide and asked him what holiday he celebrates. Suneel told Hamza, "I celebrate Diwali because I am Hindu."

Hamza learned a lot that day about his friends and their religions. He understood that all his friends got gifts on their own special holidays. Hamza was looking forward to getting presents on the next Eid.